INFLUENCE X: HOW SOCIAL MEDIA TRANSFORMS POLITICAL POWER

COMPENDIUM OF ANALYSIS

Jose Esteban Oria

JOSE ESTEBAN ORIA

Influence X: How Social Media Transforms Political Power

DEDICATION

To all those who seek the truth behind the screen,

To those who believe in the transformative power of words and critical thinking,

And especially to those who, in the digital age, fight for a more transparent, fair and connected politics with the people.

This book is for you.

GRATITUDE

I would like to express my deepest gratitude to all those who have contributed directly or indirectly to the production of this book. First of all, I thank each reader who has devoted their time and attention to these pages, seeking to understand the complexity of digital influence in our political age.

To my colleagues and mentors in the fields of communication and politics, thank you for your constructive criticism, for the discussions that have enriched this work, and for the shared knowledge that has shaped my ideas. Your experience and perspective have been invaluable.

Special recognition goes to X's active users, whose engagement and participation on the platform have provided the empirical material for this analysis. Without their interaction, this study would not have the depth it now possesses.

Thanks to my family and friends, who have supported me unconditionally, offering not only their encouragement but also their patience during the moments of immersion in this project. Their emotional support has been my anchor.

To the researchers, journalists and activists who fight every day for transparency and truth in the digital age, I thank you for your tireless work that inspires many, including me, to seek a deeper understanding of how technology influences our lives.

Finally, to technology itself, for being a canvas for our ideas, a channel for our voices, and a mirror of our society. Thank you for opening new avenues of communication and for the constant challenge of understanding and using your power responsibly.

Each of these contributions has been crucial to bringing this book to life, and for that, my gratitude is immense.

INDEX

PREFACE

In a world where communication has become as essential as the air we breathe, the X platform, formerly known as Twitter, has emerged not only as a space for the exchange of ideas, but as a catalyst for political change in Venezuela. This book, "The Power of X and the Transformation of Political Communication in Venezuela," is a journey through how this social network has redefined power, influence, and mobilization in a country marked by polarization and information censorship.

My interest in writing about this topic arose from direct observation of how X has altered the way Venezuelans interact with politics. In a country where opposition voices have desperately sought ways to be heard, X has transformed into a digital trench where the battle for truth and freedom of expression is fought daily.

This book is not just about technology or social media; it is a story about human resilience, communicative ingenuity, and the fight for democracy in modern times. Here, we explore how political figures and activists have used X to overcome regime-imposed barriers, how emerging leaders have gained ground thanks to their ability to connect with audiences on a personal level, and how the platform has given voice to those who were previously silenced.

Throughout these pages, we will demystify the idea that political power lies only in large numbers of followers. Instead, we will reveal how interaction, authenticity of message and the ability to generate conversation are the true indicators of influence in the digital age.

This preface is an invitation to reflect on how the digital tools we have at our disposal can transform our political reality. It is an invitation to recognize the power of each tweet, each retweet and each comment in building a freer and more democratic future for Venezuela.

I hope this book will serve not only to understand the X phenomenon in Venezuela but also to inspire others to use technology in innovative and courageous ways in the search for justice and social change.

In this spirit of hope and commitment, I welcome you to "Influence X: How Social Media Transforms Political Power."

INTRODUCTION

Elon Musk: "What many traditional journalists don't like is being on the same platform as ordinary citizens, they don't like their voice to have the same weight. They are very angry, we must promote citizen journalism, without filters."

The book " **"X INFLUENCE: HOW SOCIAL MEDIA TRANSFORMS POLITICAL POWER"** unravels how platform X, formerly known as Twitter, has reconfigured the political landscape in Venezuela. Here, X is not just a social network; it has evolved into a decisive tool for the dissemination of political messages, citizen mobilization, and the formation of public opinion in a country where traditional communication has been controlled or censored.

The first chapter, "The X Phenomenon in Global Politics," shows how X has democratized communication, allowing political leaders and ordinary citizens to compete directly with mass media. International examples are highlighted, such as Donald Trump, who used the platform to build his political narrative without intermediaries. In Venezuela, figures such as María Corina Machado have taken advantage of X to surpass the reach of official channels, connecting directly with the population and generating a tangible impact in the political arena.

The text explores how in Venezuela, X has become an information battlefield where authenticity and engagement are more important than the number of followers. The platform has allowed a group of influencers and content creators to set the tone in political discourse, mobilizing the audience with resonant content. This change in the dynamics of communication has made it clear that true reach is not measured only by numerical popularity, but by genuine interaction with the content.

Furthermore, the book introduces the concept of " Technopoliticians ," new leaders who emerge through their ability to use X and other digital platforms to directly influence the public. This new breed of leadership not only challenges traditional leaders but also paves the way for a generation of politicians who understand and harness digital technology for their own ends.

The analysis extends to how X's algorithm prioritizes engagement over follower count, which has resulted in a significant shift in the perception of influence. A methodology for evaluating digital influence is detailed, based not only on audience size but on the quality and impact of engagement, adjusting the value based on the type of content – original, curated or promotional.

In conclusion, "The Power of X and the Transformation of Political Communication in Venezuela" is not only a study of technological change but also an exploration of how this phenomenon is shaping politics, society and the democratization of information in a context as particular as the Venezuelan one. This book offers a critical and detailed look at the power of social media in contemporary politics.

.

MOMENTS FROM MY POLITICAL AND
ACADEMIC LIFE THAT I WANT TO SHARE

José Esteban Oria was invited to the Globovisión newscast by Derek Blanco

José Esteban Oria accompanies Dr. Miguel Henrique Otero at the Congress of Political Scientists

Jose Esteban Oria invited by Macky Arenas Globovision

José Esteban Oria inaugurating the Expotic

José Esteban Oria giving a lecture in the National Assembly chamber at the Congress of Political Science students

...

JOSE ESTEBAN ORIA

José Esteban Oria and authorities of the Rectorate of the Central University of Venezuela at the Opening of the Technological Congress

José Esteban Oria with his students in the classrooms of the Central University of Venezuela

José Esteban Oria opening the Android Meeting

Attendance of people at the Android Meeting event held in the auditorium of the newspaper El Nacional

Esteban Oria Guest on Julio Cesar Pineda's TV show

Jose Esteban Oria inaugurating the e-government conference

THE X PHENOMENON IN POLITICS

By Esteban Oria -

X, formerly known as Twitter, is no longer just a social network. Today, it is a tool that is transforming the way politics communicates, how citizens are informed and how movements for change are generated in the world.

In the past, large networks like CNN, BBC or Telemundo had a monopoly on information and the power to influence public opinion. Today, X is democratising communication. Anyone with a relevant message can compete directly with these giants.

An emblematic example is Donald Trump, who used the platform to build his narrative without intermediaries. His posts mobilized millions of people and played a key role in his return to the political scene and in his electoral victory.

This shift is also reflected in other countries. Take Venezuela, where opposition leaders like Maria Corina Machado have used X to connect directly with people, going beyond the reach of the regime's official channels.

The impact in Venezuela: between leaders and propaganda

In Venezuela, X has gone from being a simple social network to becoming an information battlefield. Leaders like María Corina Machado have reached millions of views, consolidating their relevance in the political debate. In contrast, figures like Nicolás Maduro rely on thousands of accounts of their officials to inflate their numbers in comments and RTs, showing the lack of authenticity of their reach.

A key difference emerges here: true reach is not measured in followers, but in the genuine impact of the message. While opposition influencers manage to mobilize ideas and generate discussion, regime figures lack credibility and real resonance.

During the presidential elections, content related to the campaign of Edmundo González and María Corina Machado received many more views than content linked to Maduro. This type of relationship is comparable to the number of votes Edmundo received: a post in favor of Edmundo generated three or four times more interest than one about Maduro, a behavior similar to that seen at the polls, where Edmundo outperformed Maduro by tripling his vote.

The X platform became a showcase for the pro-freedom influencers ' ideas, which connected deeply with users. In addition, the content produced by influencers supporting Edmundo generated much more reach, retweets , and comments than that generated by Maduro and his team. This infuriated the regime, which accused X of a virtual coup, but there was no real justification behind these accusations; it was just an excuse to justify the repression that even included the closure of X in Venezuela. Elon Musk got personally involved, denouncing Maduro for what he is: a dictator.

In fact, among the things that happened was a video produced by Maduro claiming that Elon Musk is satanic and is going to steal Venezuela's "wealth," while Maduro presents himself as a Christian pastor who works with "GOD." This narrative definitely ignores the reality that the real thief is Maduro. In another video, Maduro says that Maria Corina Machado has a satanic pact with Elon Musk and the US church.

This was a really crazy thing Maduro did to prevent ideas from spreading through X, but it didn't stop Edmundo from easily beating him in the presidential election.

The truth is that X made it possible to reveal the true reach of Maduro and his followers, which is quite low. It also functioned as a connector between opposition leaders and the population, to the point that many of Chavez's former voters leaned towards Edmundo and Maria Corina due to the information they received from X. The public rallies of Maria Corina and Edmundo were multitudinous, and all those invitations ran through X's network. That is the freedom that Maduro wanted to block.

But this network also allowed the emergence of new figures on the scene. From being totally unknown to now being powerful megaphones in favor of freedom, in my case I am pleasantly surprised by what X has done with me. Before I was a columnist writing in a newspaper with my personal account with limited reach. But since I started creating video content with my own first-person image supporting Edmundo's campaign, everything changed. I reached not hundreds of thousands, but millions of views, and even after the campaign, now making content in favor of freedom and the restoration of democracy and the constitution, in total so far reaching more than 30 million so far this year and exceeding 250 thousand retweets . This is an incredible achievement, which reflects what X can offer: if you produce good content, you will be rewarded by the audience that supports you. In fact, the same thing happened when I published content on TikTok, obtaining the same growth results because the final format of the content on X is reusable on both platforms. And this is seen in many other influencers who are online producing content and have become a magnet for attraction.

I have seen new influencers in the sense of their current connotation in Venezuelan politics with a great capacity for communication, people like Emmanuel Rincón, a digital communication leader with a powerful voice aligned with María Corina's platform.

Rincón has used his platform to express critical opinions about the Venezuelan government and to support opposition movements. He is known for his direct and sometimes controversial style, which has earned him both supporters and detractors.

His influence is evident in how his posts often generate discussions and interactions on the social network. Although he is not the only one, there are other influencers like him in Venezuela who have achieved a similar presence:

o José Amalio Graterol: A communicator and political activist who has used X to offer analysis on Venezuelan politics with a critical approach towards the government.

o Miguel Ángel Rodríguez: A political analyst whose presence on X has grown due to his comments on the situation in the country and his support for the opposition.

o Sebastiana Barráez : Although best known as a journalist, her activity in X has focused on security and political issues, and she has participated in the public discussion on political events, including those related to the opposition.

This network is showing a new face of the voices of communication. This democratization in X is affecting traditional media, which no longer have as much reach as the individuals who generate digital content. I understand that this is part of the objective of Elon Musk, who has said that now we are the media. The same thing happens with figures from both the regime and the opposition; both sides have been affected, and new actors have emerged who are achieving a massive reach, carrying the message of freedom, democracy and denouncing human rights violations in Venezuela.

So if X could be an invisible engine in Donald Trump's campaign, boosting his candidacy, it can also do the same anywhere in the world, just as it happened in Venezuela with Edmundo's victory.

This phenomenon is shaping a new type of leadership: a digital leadership, which reaches out directly and effectively to the masses. This phenomenon could begin to compete with traditional leaders and overthrow them, giving way to what we could call the new political generation: the Technopoliticians .

LET'S TALK ABOUT THE ALGORITHM AND ITS CHANGES

By Esteban Oria

Based on the discussion about how X's new algorithm prioritizes engagement and interaction over follower count, here is a rough suggestion for assigning percentages to each metric in the context of evaluating an influencer 's influence on X:

- **Followers:** 10%

    o   While having a large following can provide a foundation and potential for reach, follower count alone is not a direct indicator of real influence or impact. Many followers can be passive, and the algorithm has been shown to give less weight to this factor compared to engagement.

- **RTs , Comments and Likes (Content Indicators):** 80%

    o   **RTs (Retweets):** 40% - Retweets are crucial because they increase the visibility of content beyond the original follower base, indicating that the message is valuable or resonant enough for others to share.

    o   **Comments:** 20% - Comments reflect a deeper level of engagement as they indicate that the audience is not only viewing the content but is also willing to interact with it, possibly debating, discussing or expanding on the topic.

    o   **Likes:** 10% - While likes are a more passive form of interaction, they are still an indicator that content has been well received and can contribute to X's recommendation algorithm.

○ Views : 10% - These are an indicator of the audience's first impression and initial interest. Although they do not represent direct interaction, they are essential because without views, there can be no interaction. They reflect the content's ability to capture the audience's attention at first.

Reason for this Distribution:

- The high weighting towards RTs , comments and likes reflects the importance that the current X algorithm places on active interaction with the content. This not only increases the visibility of the post but also suggests that the content is relevant to the platform's community.

- Followers are considered but with less weight because they do not guarantee engagement ; however, they are necessary for interactions to occur in the first place.

These percentages are approximate and could vary depending on how algorithms evolve and how specific the objectives of a campaign or analysis are. In addition, the effectiveness of an influencer also depends on qualitative factors such as authenticity, relevance of the content to the target audience, and the ability to create meaningful trends or conversations.

When it comes to evaluating social media content, the type of post can be classified into several categories based on effort, originality, and the value it brings to the audience. Here is a breakdown:

1. **Original Content Creators (OCCs):** These are the people who generate their own content. Take Esteban Oria, for example, who does video analysis. The value here lies in the originality, investment of time, and specialization of the content. CCOs tend to have a higher value because they demonstrate unique skills, specialized knowledge, and an engagement with their audience

that goes beyond simply sharing or commenting on the work of others.

2. **Commentators and Content Curators (CCC):** These are those who, rather than creating original content, focus on sharing and commenting on the content of others. Their value is based on their ability to add value through analysis, opinions, or summaries. Although they do not produce the initial content, their interpretation or critique can be very valuable, especially if they are experts on the subject or have a unique perspective.

3. **Content Promoters (CP):** This category includes those who primarily share content without adding much commentary or analysis of their own. Their value may be lower in terms of originality or intellectual input, but let's not underestimate the value of content curation. They can be crucial to spreading relevant information and trends, acting as a filter for their audience.

Digital Influence Classification: Added Value by Type of Content on Social Networks

A CCO in this context is not limited to simply reproducing existing information or content, but adds layers of value through:

- **Research and Scriptwriting:** Writes your own script based on research or personal experience, which requires a high level of preparation and specialization in the subject matter.

- **Production and Post-Production:** Manages the production process, from filming to editing, demonstrating technical skills in camera handling, video editing, and sound editing.

- **Format Innovation:** Use advanced editing techniques, such as incorporating music and visual effects, to make content more engaging and professional.

- **Distribution and Strategy:** Decide how and where to publish your content, which may involve a marketing or audience engagement strategy.

Value Added Metric for Influencers

These types of creators are especially valuable in the digital ecosystem because they provide new and unique content, which can be educational, informative, entertaining, or a mix of these elements.

Category	Description	Effort	Originality	Engagement	Knowledge	Base Value	Increase in added value
CCO (Original Creator)	Generate your own content, video analysis, etc.	High	High	High	High	100%	+30%
CCC (Curator/Commentator)	Share and comment on third-party content, adding analysis or critique.	Half	Half	Medium-High	Half	100%	+20%
PC (Content Promoter)	He mainly shares content without much	Low	Low	Low-Medium	Low	100%	+10%

	analysis of his own.					

Explanation of the Columns:

- **Effort:** Reflects the work and time invested in creating or curating the content.

- **Originality:** The degree to which the content is unique or created by the influencer .

- **Engagement :** The ability to generate interaction with the audience.

- **Knowledge:** The level of specialization or expertise reflected in the content.

- **Base Value:** Represents the standard value of a post or the influencer 's base rate .

- **Increase for Added Value:** Additional percentage that can be

Value by category

- **CCO** : An additional 50% is added to the total calculated value.

- **CCC** : An additional 25% is added to the total calculated value.

- **PC** : An additional 10% is added to the total calculated value.

EVALUATING THE VALUE OF INFLUENCE ON SOCIAL NETWORKS

Introduction:

In the vast ecosystem of social media, the value of a user or content creator is not simply measured by the number of followers. Real influence is built through the interaction and engagement that said user generates. In this chapter, we propose a comprehensive formula to quantify this influence value, adapted for social network X, which considers not only the follower base but also the depth of interaction with the shared content.

The Digital Influence Value Formula:

To calculate the **Total Influence Value** of a user in X, the following formula is proposed:

$$\text{Total Influence Value} = (\text{Followers} \times 0.10) + (\text{RTs} \times 0.40) + (\text{Comments} \times 0.30) + (\text{Likes} \times 0.10) + (\text{Views} \times 0.10)$$

Variables and Weights:

- **Followers:** Represent 10% of the total value, indicating the potential for reach, although not necessarily active interaction.

- **RTs (Retweets):** Weighing in at 40%, retweets are crucial as they amplify the reach of content, indicating its value or resonance to be shared.

- **Comments:** Scored at 30%, these reflect deeper engagement , suggesting the content has generated discussion or reflection.

- **Like:** At 10%, although they are a more passive form of interaction, they indicate approval and contribute to the visibility of the content.

- **Views:** Also at 10%, views represent the first impression and initial interest in the content.

Content Category Settings (BCC, BCC, PC):

To recognize the variety of impact that content can have, we propose additional adjustments based on content classification:

- **CCO (Conversational Online Content):** Adds an additional 50% to the Total Influence Value, recognizing its potential to generate debate or trend.

- **CCC (Shared Knowledge Content):** Adds an additional 25%, focused on educational or informative content.

- **PC (Cause Promotion):** Increases the value by 10%, for content intended to promote social or commercial causes.

Application Example:

- Followers: $38,000 \times 0.10 = 3,800$

- RTs : $2,000 \times 0.40 = 800$

- Comments: $1,500 \times 0.30 = 450$

- Likes: $5,000 \times 0.10 = 500$

- Views: $1,800,000 \times 0.10 = 180,000$

Adding all these values:

Total Influence Value = 3,800 + 800 + 450 + 500 + 180,000 = 185,550

Now, we apply the adjustment for content classified as CCO (Original Content Creator):

Total CCO Value = Total Influence Value × 1.50

Total CCO Value = 185,550 × 1.50

Total CCO Value = 278,325 }

Therefore, the total result of this calculation is:

- **Total Influence Value** : 185,550

- **Total CCO Value : 278,325**

Conclusion:

This formula and methodology offer a valuable tool for authors, marketers , and social media analysts looking to measure influence more accurately, considering engagement and not just follower base. By applying these calculations, one can gain a more nuanced view of digital impact and adjust content strategies accordingly.

This approach allows you to present the formula in a way that is both accessible to beginners on the topic and detailed for those with prior knowledge – ideal for a book on social media analytics or digital marketing.

Engagement Rate

The formula for calculating the **Engagement Rate** (Engagement Rate) based on the number of followers would be:

Engagement Rate = (Total Interactions / Number of Followers) × 100

Where "Total Interactions" includes likes , comments, shares, saves , clicks, and any other action users may take with the content. Multiplying by 100 turns the result into a percentage, which is a standard way of expressing this metric in social media analytics.

This formula helps you understand how well an account's content resonates with its audience by normalizing interactions by that account's audience size. That is, it's not just about how many interactions you get, but what percentage of your audience is engaging with your content.

List of influencers from the sample population

Author's note: I want to clarify that the table we've created is based on data from posts that are pinned on each user's X account. These pinned posts are often chosen because they represent the most impactful or meaningful content for the user, which may not be representative of their average or typical performance on the platform.

It is important to note that:

- Pinned Posts tend to be those that users consider their best posts, most popular, or those they want to see more.
- Data for these posts may show a much higher number of interactions and views than is typical for the account's daily or regular content.
- do not necessarily correspond to the reality of the account in terms of daily engagement or the effectiveness of each post. For example, a pinned post may have accumulated a large amount of interactions due to its relevance at a specific time, but that does not necessarily reflect the standard engagement rate or reach of other posts.

These calculations should therefore be interpreted with the understanding that they are a snapshot of a particular point in time and not necessarily a measure of the account's ongoing influence or engagement . To get a more accurate and detailed view of digital influence, it would be necessary to analyse a broader period of activity, looking at the average performance of multiple posts.

1. **Enrique Marquez** : 24.63%

2. **Esteban Oria** : 10.79%

3. **Liliana Franco** : 8.97%

4. **Maria Corina Machado** : 6.34%

5. **Edmundo Gonzalez** (second entry): 5.70%

6. **Orlando Avendano** : 4.39%

7. **Pedro Urruchurtu Noselli** : 3.73%

8. **Barry cartaya** : 3.50%

9. **Emmanuel Rincon** : 1.61%

10. **Andres Izarra** : 2.13%

11. **Juan Barreto** : 2.19%

12. **Emanuel Figueroa** : 2.44%

13. **Alejandro Rondon** : 4.89%

14. **Helena Villar** : 2.28%

15. **Jose V Carrasquero A** : 1.59%

16. **Elias ? z ?q ??** : 1.59%

17. **King Lopez Rivas** : 0.97%

18. **Indira Urbaneja** : 0.96%

19. **Juan Pablo Guanipa** : 0.96%

20. **peter karvajalino** : 0.99%

21. **Orlenys Ortiz** : 0.81%

22. **Sebastiana Barráez** : 0.75%

23. **Edmundo Gonzalez** : 2.74%

24. **Eligio Rojas** : 0.63%

25. **Pedro Infante A.** : 0.52%

26. **Nicolas Maduro** : 0.52%

27. **Delsa Solorzano** : 0.35%

28. **Carla Angola TV** : 0.36%

29. **Diosdado Cabello R** : 0.38%

30. **Jorge Rodriguez** : 0.38%

31. **Henry Ramos Allup** : 0.11%

32. **Patricia Poleo** : 0.13%

33. **Norbey A, Marín G.** : 1.63%

34. **Graciela Requena** : 1.45%

35. **Nicmer Evans** : 0.43%

36. **Julio Borges** : 0.01%

37. **Cesar Miguel Rondon** : 0.003%

38. **Leopoldo Lopez** : 0.01%

39. **Juan Guaidó** : 0.04%

40. **Madelein Garcia** : 0.27%

41. **Larissa Costas** : 0.07%

42. **Eduardo Bittar** : 1.22%

IMPACT OF THE NEW FORMULA: EVALUATING THE WEIGHTING DISTRIBUTION TO MEASURE INFLUENCE

By Esteban Oria –

In my analysis of the impact on X, I have established a weighting distribution for the different interaction indicators. Here is my take on these values:

1. Followers: 10% (0.10)

- **Justification** : While follower base is important as an indicator of reach potential, I've decided to only assign it 10% because it doesn't necessarily reflect active engagement . Many followers can be passive, and the true impact comes from how people engage with your content, not just how many people can see it.

2. RTs (Retweets): 40% (0.40)

- **Reason** : I have given significant weight to RTs because they represent a form of engagement that not only shows approval but also amplifies the reach of the content. A retweet is an act of endorsement and sharing, which is crucial to measuring real influence on a platform where the distribution of the message is vital.

3. Comments: 30% (0.30)

- **Analysis** : Comments are allocated 30% due to the value they bring in terms of deep engagement . Interacting with a comment requires time and thought, indicating a higher level of engagement than simply liking or retweeting . This reflects a more significant impact on the conversation and debate.

4. Like: 10% (0.10)

- **Explanation** : Although likes are a form of interaction, their impact is less compared to RTs and comments. That's why they only receive 10%. It is a sign of approval, but it does not imply the dissemination or discussion of the content like RTs or comments do.

5. Views: 10% (0.10)

- **Reflection** : Views are given the same weight as likes because, while they are crucial to the initial reach of content, they do not necessarily indicate significant engagement. This weight is given in recognition that without views there is no possibility of engagement, but the true impact of influence is measured more by the actions users take after viewing the content.

General Opinion:

- This distribution reflects an understanding that on X, influence is not measured just by who has the most followers, but by how users interact with the content. The high weighting of RTs and comments suggests that content that generates discussion, is shared and amplified, has a greater impact on public opinion or the promotion of ideas.

- By giving less weight to followers and views, you avoid bias towards accounts that may have high visibility but not necessarily high engagement .
- This methodology helps to identify true influencers, those who not only have an audience but also mobilize, educate or entertain them effectively.

The key is to give more weight to real interactions (like RTs) and less to followers. Here is the adjusted formula:

1. **Followers** : 10% (0.10)

2. **RTs (Retweets)** : 40% (0.40)

3. **Comments** : 30% (0.30)

4. **Like** : 10% (0.10)

5. **Views:** 10% (0.10)

The adjusted formula would be:

Total Value = (Followers × 0.10) + (RTs × 0.40) + (Comments × 0.30) + (Likes × 0.10) + (Views × 0.10)

Why make this change?

By giving 90% weight to RTs and only 10% to followers, we prioritize the real impact that the content has. If a tweet is retweeted many times, it means that it is being shared and therefore reaching more people organically. This reflects how the content is actually distributed, not just how many followers an account has. This makes much more sense in the new era of X, where content engagement and resonance are key to increasing its reach, much more than the size of the account's audience.

Pros of this formula:

1. **Greater emphasis on real engagement** : RTs carry a much higher weight, meaning content that actually resonates and is shared effectively will be favored by the algorithm.

2. **Alignment with current algorithm** : X's algorithm gives preference to RTs because they allow content to spread beyond the account's direct audience. This allows content to spread more organically and effectively.

Cons of the formula:

1. **Less value to the follower base** : By reducing the weight of followers to 10%, a large follower base, while still valuable, has a smaller impact on the bottom line. This is true even if the follower base can be an important starting point for initial visibility.

2. **Possible bias towards small but viral accounts** : Accounts with fewer followers, but which generate a high volume of interactions (RTs), could be rated higher than an account with a large following but less engagement. This highlights the importance of content quality and its ability to engage an audience, rather than just the number of followers.

Example with the new values :
- **Followers:** $38,000 \times 0.10 = 3,800$

- **RTs :** $2,000 \times 0.40 = 800$

- **Comments:** $1,500 \times 0.30 = 450$

- **Likes:** $5,000 \times 0.10 = 500$

- **Views:** $1,800,000 \times 0.10 = 180,000$

Adding all these values:

Total Value=3,800+800+450+500+180,000

Total Value=185,550

Now, if we apply the additional adjustments for different impact categories:

Total Value CCO=Total Value+(Total Value×0.50)

Total CCO Value=185,550+(185,550×0.50)

Total CCO Value=185,550+92,775

Total CCO Value=278,325

Conclusion:

This change in formula reflects how X (and similar platforms) values quality and resonance of content over simply having a large follower base. As interactions and engagement become more important, creators who manage to generate authentic and shareable conversations have a much greater opportunity to achieve greater reach, regardless of the size of their audience.

Adjusted Table of Influencers According to Their Potential (Weighting by Engagement)

Type of Influencer	Followers Rank 10%	Engagement Rate 90%	RT and Comments	Audience	Potential Impact	Characteristics	Cost	Social networks
Nano-Influencers	1K - 10K	5-10%	High	Very Faithful	Hypersegmented Niche	Close community, high interaction	Low	Instagram, TikTok
Micro-Influencers	10K - 100K	3-8%	Very High	Faithful	Segmented Niche	Experts in specific topics, high confidence	Moderate	Instagram, YouTube,

								TikTok
Macro-Influencers	100K - 1M	1.5-3%	Moderate	Wide	Significant Scope	References in their field, good price-impact ratio	Moderate to High	Instagram, YouTube
Mega-Influencers	1M - 5M	0.5-1.5%	Low to Moderate	Very Wide	Massive Reach	Digital celebrities, global reach	High	Instagram, YouTube, X
Celebrities / All-Stars	>5M	<0.5%	Low	Global	Massive Reach	Public figures with great recognition	Very High	

Calculating Engagement Rate (ER) :

- ○ **General Formula** : Engagement Rate = (Total Interactions / Reach) * 100

  - ▪ Where interactions include likes , comments, retweets (in X), and views (on platforms like YouTube or TikTok if they are considered relevant for the calculation of engagement).

- ○ **Total Interactions** : Sum of likes , comments, retweets , and views. However, for simplicity and to focus on direct interaction, we could exclude views from the engagement calculation , focusing on likes , comments , and retweets .

Weighting by Interaction Type :

- o Not all engagement is equal; a comment often carries more weight than a like . You might assign a higher value to comments, for example, considering that a comment is equivalent to 2 or 3 likes in terms of engagement .

Adjustment in Table :

- o **Follower Rank** : Maintain, but emphasize that it is less relevant to engagement .

- o **Engagement (80%)** : Change to " Engagement Rate " calculated according to the proposed formula.

- o **Audience** : It could be defined not only by the number but by the quality of the following, that is, how engaged the audience is with the influencer 's content .

- o **Potential Impact** : Evaluate not only by reach but by the ability to generate actions (buy, share, comment).

- o **Features** : Include the quality of engagement (authenticity, interaction, response to brands).

- o **Cost** : Adjust based on the value of the engagement , not just the number of followers.

- o **Social Media** : Keep, but consider that platform type affects engagement (e.g. TikTok and Instagram tend to have higher engagement rates than others).

Categories

Retweet (RT) ranges to classify influence on platform X because they reflect different levels of reach and engagement that I have observed throughout my analysis. Here is my first-person justification:

Emerging Voices (50 – 150 RTs): I've included this category to recognize early-stage influencers , those with limited reach but clear growth potential. I've noticed that even with RTs between 50 and 150, these individuals are beginning to make a mark in very specific niches or local communities. This range shows early and promising engagement with their audience, even if it's small.

Local Legends (150 - 500 RTs): I've chosen this range because, in my experience, influencers who receive between 150 and 500 RTs are those who have a significant but limited impact to their specific locality or niche. I've seen how these people can mobilize their community, whether for local events or to discuss very specific topics. This level of engagement shows real engagement from the audience, even if their reach doesn't extend beyond their immediate circle.

Regional Risers (500 - 1,500 RTs): I've decided that this range is appropriate for those influencers with a broader impact within a specific region or sector. My observations indicate that when a post receives between 500 and 1,500 RTs , the content is resonating with an audience beyond the local scope, but still within a defined geographic or thematic context. I've noticed that this amount of RTs can influence regional trends or the opinion of a group of people with common interests.

National Narrators (1,500 - 3,000 RTs): I've set this range for influencers who are just starting to gain influence on a national level. I've seen that when a post reaches between 1,500 and 3,000 RTs , it becomes a topic of discussion on a large scale within a country. This amount of engagement indicates that the content is being widely shared and discussed, giving these individuals the ability to shape the national narrative on certain topics.

Global Gurus (3,000 - 6,000 RTs): I've chosen this range because it reflects an influence that goes beyond national borders. I've observed that when RTs reach this level, the content is impacting a global audience, opening conversations across different cultures and societies. This range shows that the influencer can connect with people all over the world, influencing cultural trends or international debates.

Iconic Influencers (+6,000 RTs): I've defined this range for influencers who have a massive and almost instantaneous impact globally. More than 6,000 RTs are rare and mean that the content has captured global attention in an extraordinary way. I've seen how these numbers can change policies, start movements, or alter public opinion on a global scale. I decided to use this threshold because it reflects a power of influence that only a few can achieve, marking a significant change in the public sphere.

These ranges are the result of my analysis of engagement data on X, combined with my understanding of how influence manifests on the platform. I've considered both the number of RTs and the context in which they occur, ensuring that each category reflects a realistic scale of impact.

Category	Engagement Rate (RT per post)	Proposed Name	Characteristics	Potential Impact
Emerging Voices	50 - 150 RT	Micro Influencers	Early-stage influencers with limited reach but growth potential. Experts in very specific niches or with an engaged local audience.	They can start trends in very small communities, offer fresh perspectives, or be pioneers on emerging topics.
Local Legends	150 - 500 RT	Community Catalysts	Influencers who have a strong impact locally or within specific	They can influence trends or changes in small communities or on

			niches. They have an engaged audience but limited reach.	very specific topics.
Regional Risers	500 - 1,500 RT	Niche Notables	These influencers have a broader reach than 'Local Legends', reaching regional audiences. Their content is relevant and frequently shared.	Able to mobilize or educate audiences within a particular interest or broader geographic area.
National Narrators	1,500 - 3,000 RT	Trendsetters	These influencers have a significant capacity to define or influence national trends. Their opinions and content are widely shared and discussed.	Their influence extends across a country, allowing them to shape public opinion, influence national debates and, in some cases, affect politics or public policy.
Global Gurus	3,000 - 6,000 RT	Cultural Catalysts	Influencers in this category have an influence that transcends national borders, reaching global audiences. Their content is often	They can spark global movements, influence international politics, or change cultural perceptions. Their content has the power to connect

			of international interest.	different cultures and generate global debates.
Iconic Influencers	+6,000 RT	Global Game Changers	These are the influencers with the ability to create a massive and almost instant impact on a global level. Their content is not only widely shared but can also provoke significant changes in public opinion, policies, or even popular culture on a global scale.	They have the influence to start or stop global campaigns, to influence political decisions.

1. **Category** : Defines the level of influence of influencers based on their reach and the type of audience they impact. From those who operate in a very specific or local context, to those who have a global impact.

2. **Engagement Rate (RT per post)** : This is a quantitative indicator of the engagement or interaction that an influencer can generate with their content. It is measured by the number of retweets (RT) that a post receives, which reflects the audience's interest and willingness to share the content with others.

3. **Proposed Name** : Refers to a creative or descriptive designation given to each category of influencers to highlight their particular role or impact on society or their specific niche. For example, "

Community " Catalysts " for Local Legends , suggests their role as catalysts for changes or trends within local communities.

4. **Characteristics** : Describes the qualities and reach of influencers within each category. Include the type of audience they attract, the content they produce, and how this content is received and shared. For example, " Trendsetters " (National Trendsetters) Narrators are known for their ability to define or influence trends at a national level, which means content that resonates widely and is relevant to a diverse audience within a country.

5. **Potential Impact** : This concept assesses the effect that influencers can have on their environment, whether at a local, regional, national or global level. It includes their ability to generate change, influence public opinion, initiate debates, or even affect policies. For example, the "Global Game" Changers

Why categories start at 50 retweets and not less

In my book, I've acknowledged that reaching those levels of Retweets (RT) is not easy, even for leaders with a million followers. Here's my justification for including these ranges, considering the difficulty and reality of engagement in X:

The Difficulty of Reaching 50 RTs: I have observed that even for those with a large number of followers, getting 50 RTs per post is a remarkable achievement. This is due to several factors:

- Engagement vs. Followers: Not all followers engage with every post. The number of followers does not guarantee high engagement , as it depends on the relevance of the content, the time of posting, and the competition in the followers' feed . I have noticed that many followers can be passive, just watching without interacting.

- Content Quality and Relevance: I have seen that only content that resonates deeply with the audience, that is timely, or that generates a strong emotional reaction, achieves these levels of RT. It is not just a matter of having followers, but of connecting with them at the right time with the right message.

Why So Many People Are Left Out:

- The Saturation Factor: The platform is saturated with content. I have observed that even large media outlets do not reach 500 RTs per post due to information overload. X's audience is bombarded with so many posts that only the most impactful or viral ones capture the attention necessary to reach those numbers.

- Nature of X: I've learned that X, as a platform, favors content that generates conversation, controversy, or novel information. Many publications, even from major outlets, fail to stand out if they don't meet these criteria.

- Algorithm and Visibility: X's algorithm plays a crucial role. I've noticed that not all content is equally visible to all followers, depending on past engagement, interests, and other factors. This means that even with a million followers, only a fraction of them might see and react to a post.

Justification of Ranks:

- I have established these ranks not just based on follower numbers, but on the real, measurable impact of the content. I have seen that these RT levels reflect genuine influence, not just in terms of visibility, but in terms of mobilization, education and change.

- I've decided to include these ranges to highlight that influence on X is not measured by the number of followers alone, but by the quality and impact of the interaction. This leaves out many with large follower numbers but low engagement , focusing on those who really move the needle in the digital conversation.

These ranks are therefore a way of measuring the effectiveness and true reach of an influencer in the context of a platform where attention is a scarce and valuable resource.

1. **Relevance of Engagement** :

   o   Reaching 50 retweets per post indicates a significant
       level of engagement, proving that the content resonates
       enough to motivate followers to share it. This reflects an
       active connection with the audience, which is crucial to
       measuring the true influence of an account.

   o   Furthermore, this level of engagement is an indicator
       that the influencer 's impact transcends their follower
       base, reaching new audiences through retweets .

2. **Differentiation and Quality** :

   o   Setting 50 retweets as a starting point filters out the
       influencers who are truly making an impact compared to
       those with lower engagement numbers, who might not
       be attracting an engaged audience.

   o   This helps focus analysis on accounts that produce
       relevant and valuable content, emphasizing quality over
       quantity.

3. **Statistical Relevance** :

   o   In the context of platforms like X, where millions of
       posts are generated daily, 50 retweets represent a high
       enough number to consider that the content has captured
       attention at a relevant level.

   o   This threshold also minimizes noise from small or
       inactive accounts that could result in lower engagement
       without real impact.

4. **Segmentation Strategy** :

   o This criterion helps categorize influencers into groups
   that really generate value for marketing campaigns,
   political communication, or dissemination strategies.

   o An influencer who exceeds this threshold has a greater
   chance of converting their digital impact into tangible
   results, whether in sales, votes or positioning.

5. **Perception of Influence** :

   o Retweets reflect how content circulates and is amplified.
   Starting at 300 ensures that categories are associated
   with accounts that achieve a perception of real influence,
   which is important for both brands and communication
   strategies .

Conclusion:

Setting 50 retweets as the initial measurement point ensures that
influencers included in these categories have a minimum level of
relevance, engagement and amplification capacity, ensuring that they are
significant actors within the X ecosystem.

REASONS FOR NOT INCLUDING VIEWS IN THE ENGAGEMENT RATE CALCULATION

By Esteban Oria –

In my analysis of influence and engagement on X, I have decided to exclude views from the core engagement rate calculations . Here are the reasons behind this decision:

1. Differentiation between Visibility and Interaction:

- **Views vs. Active Engagement** : Views indicate how many times a piece of content has been shown, which is a visibility metric, not an engagement metric. Genuine engagement is manifested through actions like RTs , comments, and likes, which represent active interaction with the content.

2. Quality of Interaction:

- **Meaningful Interactions** : My focus is on interactions that demonstrate real engagement on the part of the user. While a view may be passive (a user may have simply viewed the content while browsing), actions like RTs and comments indicate a much more significant level of interest and participation.

3. Metric Inflation:

- **Repeated Views** : Views may include multiple views by the same user, which can artificially inflate the number without necessarily indicating higher engagement . This does not reflect the actual influence or ability of a piece of content to generate action or discussion.

4. Content Strategies:

- **Promoting Quality Over Quantity** : By not counting views in engagement , creators are incentivized to produce content that motivates audiences to actively interact, not just watch. This encourages the creation of higher quality, more impactful content.

5. Consistency with the Purpose of Engagement :

- **Engagement as Interaction** : Engagement rate should measure a piece of content's ability to generate a response from the audience. Views, while important for initial reach, do not capture this interaction. Instead, the metrics I've selected (RTs , comments, likes) are direct indications of how the audience is actively responding to the content.

6. Comparative Analysis:

- **Fair Comparability** : Excluding views allows for a fairer comparison between influencers and content, focusing on actual impact rather than mere exposure. This helps identify who is truly influencing the conversation and not just who has content that is being viewed.

7. Alignment with the X Algorithm:

- **Algorithm and Relevance** : While views can help content get seen, X's algorithm also focuses on how users interact with content after viewing it. Active interactions are what really drive long-term visibility and ranking of content on the platform.

For these reasons, I have decided that views are not part of the engagement rate calculation . The goal is to capture the essence of influence that goes beyond mere exposure, focusing on the ability of an individual or content to mobilize, educate, or change perceptions through meaningful interaction.

JOSE ESTEBAN ORIA

REASONS FOR THE FOLLOWER-BASED ENGAGEMENT RATE FORMULA

By Esteban Oria -

In the methodology I have developed to calculate the Engagement Rate in X, I have decided to divide all the interaction indicators (RTs , comments, likes) by the number of followers and multiply the result by 100. Here are the fundamental reasons behind this formula:

1. Normalization of Engagement :

- **Standardization** : Dividing interactions by the number of followers normalizes engagement , allowing for fair comparisons between accounts of different sizes. This means that influence isn't simply measured by the number of interactions, but by how those interactions relate to the creator's potential audience.

2. Quality over Quantity:

- **Engagement Relevance** : By dividing by the number of followers, the emphasis is on the quality of engagement rather than the quantity. A small account with a high percentage of engaged followers may be more influential than a large account with a low engagement percentage.

3. Proportional Perspective:

- **Active Audience Proportion** : Multiplying by 100 converts the result into a percentage, which provides a clear perspective on how large a portion of the audience is interacting with the content. This offers a measure of how much of the potential audience is actually engaged with the message.

4. Comparability:

- **Cross-Analysis** : This formula allows you to compare the engagement of influencers with very different follower bases. Without this normalization, it would be difficult to determine whether an influencer with a large following but low engagement has more impact than one with fewer followers but higher engagement .

5. Reflection of the Real Impact:

- **Relative Influence : The** engagement rate calculated this way reflects the actual impact of the content on its specific audience. It shows how effective an influencer is at motivating their audience to interact, which is a more accurate indicator of influence than just counting the absolute number of interactions.

6. Adaptation to the Digital Ecosystem:

- **Social Media Dynamics : In the context of X, where users can have very varied follower bases, this formula helps to understand how** engagement behaves in an environment where the relevance of content and connection with the audience are key.

7. Efficiency Metric:

- **Content Effectiveness** : Using this formula, we can evaluate the effectiveness of an influencer 's content in generating relative engagement with their follower base. This is useful for marketing campaigns, trend analysis, and digital communication strategies.

8. Simplification and Clarity:

- **Easy Understanding** : Converting interactions into a percentage makes the data more understandable and accessible for both content creators, analysts and general users of the platform.

In short, this formula is a valuable tool for measuring influence in a way that fits the reality of digital communication, focusing on the direct relationship between an influencer 's audience and their ability to generate an active and interactive response.

SOURCE OF TRUTH ABOUT THE ALGORITHM

By Esteban Oria -

There is no specific bio or article that explicitly states that X's (formerly Twitter's) algorithm is using exactly this ratio of 10% followers and 90% engagement (RTs , comments, likes , views) to prioritize content. However, there are several sources and discussions that reflect how the algorithm has evolved to emphasize engagement over mere follower count:

- ** X Algorithm: How it Works - metricool.com**This article mentions changes to the X algorithm where it is indicated that duplicate conversations will not be shown, responses will be prioritized over quotes, and more weight will be given to video and image content, suggesting a preference for active engagement .

- ** Twitter Algorithm | Tweet Deletion - tweetdelete.net**Here are tips to improve your X ranking, detailing the importance of engagement (RTs , likes , comments) to increase content visibility.

- ** Twitter Algorithm | Tweet Delete - tweetdelete.net**Discusses how the X algorithm considers user interactions (clicks , likes , replies) to personalize and recommend content, indicating that interactions are critical to ranking.

- ** Instagram Algorithm 2024: The 8 Keys +TOP - metricool.com**Although this is Instagram, it reflects a general trend in social networks towards prioritizing engagement over the number of followers, which can be extrapolated to X due to similarities in the dynamics of social platforms.

Conclusion:

The exact percentage distribution between followers and engagement that I proposed is speculation based on a synthesis of available information and an understanding of how contemporary social media algorithms tend to work. Prioritising engagement over followers is a well-documented trend, but X has not publicly disclosed the exact formula or specific weights that its algorithm uses. Therefore, any specific percentage allocation would be an interpretation or estimate of how the algorithm might work based on observations and analysis of interaction and visibility patterns on the platform.

CASE STUDY: MY TRANSFORMATION INTO AN INFLUENCER IN X

By Esteban Oria –

I have decided to use my own profile on X as a case study to understand the dynamics of influence on the platform. The information for this analysis is obtained from the sample I have compiled with the list of influencers , taking as reference data the pinned post on my profile. This data does not necessarily reflect the average of my posts, but it is a good element of analysis to understand the potential and resonance of my content.

Anchored Post Analysis:

- **Followers** : My account has 38,000 followers.
- **RTs** : I have generated 2,000 RTs with this post.
- **Comments** : I have received 1,500 comments.
- **Like** : My post has gotten 5,000 likes .
- **Views** : This post has reached 1,800,000 views.

Using the adjusted formula to calculate my Total Influence Value:

- **Total Influence Value** = $(38,000 \times 0.10) + (2,000 \times 0.40) + (1,500 \times 0.30) + (5,000 \times 0.10) + (1,800,000 \times 0.10) = 3,800 + 800 + 450 + 500 + 180,000 = \mathbf{185,550}$.

As an Original Content Creator (OCC), I apply the 50% increase:

- **Total CCO Value** = $185,550 + (185,550 \times 0.50) = 185,550 + 92,775 = \mathbf{278,325}$.

My **Engagement Rate** for this post is:

- **Total Interactions** : $2,000 + 1,500 + 5,000 = 8,500$
- **ER** = $(8,500 / 38,000) \times 100 \approx \mathbf{22.37\%}$.

Analysis of Four Recent Posts:

Now, I want to analyze four of my most recent posts to see how my influence varies:

- **Post 1** :
  - Comments: 30
  - RTs : 1,000
  - Likes: 1,000
  - Views: 26,000
- **Post 2** :
  - Comments: 328
  - RTs : 11,000
  - Likes: 15,000
  - Views: 342,000
- **Post 3** :
  - Comments: 328
  - RTs : 1,600
  - Likes: 2,000
  - Views: 201,000

Calculating Total Influence Value for Each Post:

- **Post 1** :
  - Total Value = $(38,000 \times 0.10) + (1,000 \times 0.40) + (30 \times 0.30) + (1,000 \times 0.10) + (26,000 \times 0.10) = 3,800 + 400 + 9 + 100 + 2,600 =$ **6,909** .
- **Post 2** :
  - Total Value = $(38,000 \times 0.10) + (11,000 \times 0.40) + (328 \times 0.30) + (15,000 \times 0.10) + (342,000 \times 0.10) = 3,800 + 4,400 + 98.4 + 1,500 + 34,200 =$ **44,098.4** .
- **Post 3** :
  - Total Value = $(38,000 \times 0.10) + (1,600 \times 0.40) + (328 \times 0.30) + (2,000 \times 0.10) + (201,000 \times 0.10) = 3,800 + 640 + 98.4 + 200 + 20,100 =$ **24,838.4** .

Setting for CCO :

- **Post 1 CCO** : $6{,}909 + (6{,}909 \times 0.50) = 6{,}909 + 3{,}454.5 = $ **10,363.5** .
- **Post 2 CCO** : $44{,}098.4 + (44{,}098.4 \times 0.50) = 44{,}098.4 + 22{,}049.2 = $ **66,147.6** .
- **Post 3 CCO** : $24{,}838.4 + (24{,}838.4 \times 0.50) = 24{,}838.4 + 12{,}419.2 = $ **37,257.6** .

Engagement Rate for Each Post:

- **Post 1** : $ER = ((1{,}000 + 30 + 1{,}000) / 38{,}000) \times 100 \approx $ **5.55%**
- **Post 2** : $ER = ((11{,}000 + 328 + 15{,}000) / 38{,}000) \times 100 \approx $ **69.21%**
- **Post 3** : $ER = ((1{,}600 + 328 + 2{,}000) / 38{,}000) \times 100 \approx $ **10.36%**

Summary and Conclusions:

This analysis shows that my influence varies significantly depending on the content. While the pinned post and Post 2 demonstrate a high level of engagement , indicating greater influence, other posts show more moderate engagement . This suggests that consistency in creating high-quality content is key to maintaining and increasing my impact as an influencer . My position on the "Adjusted Influencer Table " varies, but at times of high engagement like with Post 2, I could be classified as a **Global Guru** , due to the ability to generate global reach and discussion.

The variability in my recent posts reflects the reality of influence on X: it depends a lot on the relevance and timing of the content. As CCO, my goal is to maintain a high average engagement rate , ensuring that my posts are not only seen but also incite action and debate.

THE IMPACT OF CHANGES IN X: HOW THEY AFFECT TRADITIONAL LEADERS AND GIVE WAY TO NEW FIGURES IN VENEZUELAN POLITICS.

Traditional opposition leaders such as Leopoldo López and Antonio Ledezma, despite having a significant base of followers on X, are failing to generate a significant connection with the public, nor achieve the levels of interaction they used to have on the old Twitter. This phenomenon is especially striking considering the number of followers they have, which generates greater expectations about their reach and impact. For example:

- **Leopoldo López** has **2.4 million followers** , but his posts reach an average of **7 thousand views** .

- **Antonio Ledezma** has a similar performance, with **50 retweets** on average, which reflects a low impact considering his audience.

Other leaders also show low results in relation to their number of followers:

- **Julio Borges** : 1 million followers, average of **5 thousand views**
  .

- **Henry Ramos Allup** : 1.7 million followers, average of **10 thousand views** , although his best fixed post reaches **140 thousand** .

However, there are cases of better performance:

- **Eduardo Battistini** : It has an average of **50 thousand views** , with peaks exceeding **200 thousand** .

- **Pedro Urruchurtu** : Between **30,000 and 50,000 views** , with some peaks of **300,000** , probably driven by his particular situation as a political leader in exile.

On the other hand, in the ruling party, the reach on networks is also conditioned:

- **Indira Urbaneja** : Her posts range between **2,000 and 15,000 views** , despite having 40,000 followers and receiving support from accounts aligned with the regime.

- **Roi López** : With **211.5 thousand followers** , he has an average of **12 thousand views** .

- **Madelein García** : Her content has between **5,000 and 15,000 views** , although it occasionally reaches **50,000** .

The case of **Nicolás Maduro** is particular, as his posts reach between **200,000 and 500,000 views** , with peaks of millions. This is due to a strategy that involves the massive use of accounts controlled by the regime, organized comments and a constant flow of criticism that increases his visibility.

In contrast, opposition leader **María Corina Machado** stands out as the most influential on social media:

- **5.9 million followers** , an average of **600 thousand views** per post, and a pinned post with **10 million views** , doubling Maduro's best.

- **Edmundo González** , another opposition leader, also has a notable performance with between **70,000 and 100,000 views** per post, despite having less than a million followers.

Finally, influencers who support opposition leaders like María Corina also achieve good results:

- **Orlando Avendaño** : With **260 thousand followers** , he has a pinned post with **3 million views** , although most of his publications average between **6 thousand and 56 thousand views** .

- **Emmanuel Rincón** : Generates content with peaks of up to **300 thousand views** , although many posts have a more modest reach of **5 thousand to 180 thousand views** .

- **In my case, Esteban Oria's account** is performing well, with posts regularly reaching an average of 40,000 views. However, I have also achieved a wide spectrum of posts with views ranging from 100,000 to 700,000, and some have even exceeded 2 million views. In addition, I have received 21,000 likes and 11,000 retweets . These results clearly demonstrate how X is allowing my content to flow and reach a wider audience, generating a significant impact.

X is becoming a key environment to measure and understand political influence in Venezuela and the world. The numbers reflect a profound change in how people consume and participate in political discourse. Leaders and movements that do not adapt to this change will be left behind in their ability to connect with audiences.

Name	account x	followers	comments	RT	I like	views	Digital Influence Classification	New Digital Influence
Maria Corina Machado	@MariaCorinaYA	5.9M Followers	9000	91000	283000	10000000	cco	1778850.00
Emmanuel Rincon	@EmmaRincon	536.3K Followers	739	1000	3000	5000000	cco	839454.45
Nicolas Maduro	@NicolasMaduro	4.8M Followers	14000	5000	6000	2000000	cco	444000.00

Orlando Avendano	@OrlvndoA	260.1K Followers	808	3000	8000	3000000	cco	507150.15
Esteban Oria	@estebanoria	38000	1000	7000	21000	1800000	cco	278325.00
Edmundo Gonzalez	@EdmundoGU	998.7K Followers	804	11000	45000	698000	cco	225570.60
Diosdado Cabello R	@dcabellor	2.8M Followers	4000	4000	6000	521000	cco	211200.00
Edmundo Gonzalez	@EdmundoGU	998.7K Followers	372	10000	17000	328000	cco	211630.50
Carla Angola TV	@carlaangola	2.9M Followers	213	3000	7000	443	cco	193714.50
Enrique Marquez	@ENRIQUEMARQUEZP	153.4K Followers	1000	10000	26000	868000	cco	184650.00
Jorge Rodriguez	@jorgerpsuv	1.3M Followers	1000	2000	2000	254000	cco	114450.00
Leopoldo Lopez	@leopoldolopez	5.2M Followers	5	72	195	95000	cco	102742.50
Delsa Solorzano	@delsasolorzano	1.2M Followers	86	1000	3000	52000	cco	101529.00
Juan Guaidó	@jguaido	2.6M Followers	227	313	579	106000	cco	106053.00

Helena Villar	@Helena VillarRT	183.8K Followers	125	2000	2000	416000	cco	99358.20
Patricia Poleo	@PattyPoleo	1.2M Followers	298	288	1000	150000	cco	111882.00
Juan Pablo Guanipa	@JuanPGuanipa	421.5K Followers	85	1000	3000	51000	cco	69172.50
King Lopez Rivas	@RoiLopezRivas	211.6K Followers	396	651	1000	72000	cco	49067.40
Madelein Garcia	@madeleintlSUR	161.4K Followers	241	100	120	25000	cco	25817.10
Pedro Urruchurtu Noselli	@Urruchurtu	82.6K Followers	64	1000	2000	165200	cco	36804.90
Barry Cartaya	@cartayabarry	30 thousand followers	478	281	397	125000	cco	25245.00
Eduardo Bittar	@Eduardo_Bittar	113K Followers	147	467	765	206000	cco	24304.05
Indira Urbaneja	@INDIURBANEJA	44.7K Followers	19	165	258	16000	cco	5467.05
Liliana Franco	@lilianaf523	62.4K Followers	110	2000	5000	191000	ccc	84280.00

Henry Ramos Allup	@hramosallup	1.7M Followers	403	1000	2000	141000	ccc	83637.50
Sebastia Barráez	@SebastianaB	423.7K Followers	80	1000	1000	322000	ccc	68354.63
Julio Borges	@JulioBorges	1.5M Followers	9	63	70	3000	ccc	49768.75
Cesar Miguel Rondon	@cmrondon	2.9M Followers	7	27	54	5000	ccc	36817.50
Jose V Carrasquero A	@bottleshot	193.1K Followers	88	1000	2000	68000	ccc	34913.75
Andres Izarra	@AgIzarra	34.9K Followers	1	187	566	921000	ccc	118681.13
Alejandro Rondon	@ArondonFT	14.4K Followers	380	117	204	159000	ccc	23080.50
Orlenys Ortiz	@OrlenysOV	105.8K Followers	80	288	453	23000	ccc	19882.25
Nicmer Evans	@NicmerEvans	135.6K Followers	5	345	226	5000	ccc	19882.00
Emanuel Figueroa	@EmaFigueroaC	73.3K Followers	53	736	1000	40000	ccc	17416.63

INFLUENCE X: HOW THE SOCIAL NETWORK TRANSFORMS POLITICAL POWER

Graciela Requena	@gracielarequena	15.6K Followers	32	94	188	72000	ccc	13632.00
Juan Barreto	@juanbarretoc	65.9K Followers	55	459	903	20000	ccc	13257.38
Norbey A, Marín G.	@Norbey_Marin_	49.3K Followers	5	277	522	4000	ccc	7269.13
Larissa Costas	@Larissacostas	175.4K Followers	8	33	84	4000	ccc	2919.25
Peter Karvajalino	@PedroKonductaz	94.8K Followers	0	462	483	232000	cco	27791.28
Pedro Infante A.	@pinfantea	148.7K Followers	209	418	557	40000	pc	16773.57
Elias ? z ? what ??	@Elias_Cabeza	55.1K Followers	279	253	382	80000	pc	10070.61
Eligio Rojas	@ELESPINITO	30000	16	76	104	52000	pc	5770.60

Table Explanation:

This table is the result of a sample with data obtained mainly from each user's pinned post, previously compared with other posts in their account. This has been done because in some cases, the pinned post does not always faithfully reflect the usual impact of the user's posts, showing values with little congruence with respect to interactive posts. The idea of this table is to provide a perspective on the impact of each user's digital ranking on social networks.

Calculation Formula:

The digital classification is calculated using the following percentages:

- **Followers** : 10% (0.10)

- **RTs (Retweets)** : 40% (0.40)

- **Comments** : 30% (0.30)

- **Like** : 10% (0.10)

- **Views** : 10% (0.10)

Multiplication by Category:

- **CCO** : An additional 50% is added to the total calculated value.

- **CCC** : An additional 25% is added to the total calculated value.

- **PC** : An additional 10% is added to the total calculated value.

Explanation of the Formula:

- **Followers (10%)** : Represents the importance of the user's follower base, although with less weight because they do not necessarily interact with each post.

- **RTs (Retweets , 40%)** : This has the highest weight because retweets indicate a significant dissemination of the content, directly reflecting the reach and influence of the post.

- **Comments (30%)** : Comments are a strong indicator of engagement and direct participation with the content, so they carry considerable weight.

- **Like (10%)** : While likes are a sign of approval, their impact on rankings is minor due to the ease with which they can be given without further commitment.

- **Views (10%)** : Reflects how many people have seen the post, but not necessarily interacted with it, hence its moderate weight in the formula.

Multiplication by category (BCC, BCC, PC) is applied to add an additional factor based on the type of user or the context in which their digital activity is located, thus adjusting the perceived digital influence according to their role or expected impact on the specific community or sector.

REASONS WHY I BELIEVE THAT X HAS A SIGNIFICANT INFLUENCE ON POLITICS

In this chapter, I will explore the **reasons why I believe that X has a significant influence on politics** . The platform has redefined political communication through its ability to democratize access to information, offer immediacy in the dissemination of news and opinions, and change public perception of leaders. Furthermore, examples such as Donald Trump's presidential campaign in the United States illustrate how X can be a powerful vehicle for direct communication with the electoral base, without the mediation of traditional media. This analysis not only focuses on the capabilities of X but also on how it compares to other social networks such as Instagram and TikTok, highlighting why X is considered a network of excellence for politics due to its format that encourages deep debates and more meaningful interaction.

- **Simplification of Communication and Reach** : X has democratized the way information reaches people. Politicians and citizens can now communicate directly, without intermediaries, which simplifies and amplifies the political message. The platform allows a single post to reach millions, something that would be impossible or very costly in other media.

- **Speed and Immediacy** : The instantaneous nature of X allows political news, reactions and opinions to spread in real time. This is crucial in election campaigns where every minute counts in responding to events or accusations.

- **Impact on Public Perception** : The way X conveys the message can alter public perception of politicians. RTs and comments can make an issue go viral, influencing public opinion in ways that were not seen as strongly before.

- **Presidential Election Dynamics** : The case of the presidential elections in the United States is a clear example. Donald Trump used X as his main communication tool, proving that with the right media machinery, you can have a massive influence. He had X as his main platform, and this allowed him to communicate directly with his base without relying on traditional media.

Arguments for my interest in X and its relation to politics:

- **X as the Network of Excellence for Politics** : X not only allows the dissemination of ideas, but also the creation of movements, the mobilization of voters and the direct monitoring of public policies. Its format encourages discussion and the confrontation of ideas, which is essential in politics.

Comparison with Instagram and TikTok:

- **Instagram and TikTok are Important, but Not Decisive** : Both platforms have a huge cultural and social impact, but their format is more entertainment and lifestyle oriented. Politics on Instagram and TikTok tend to be more visual and less discursive, which limits the depth of political debate and discussion. Whereas X allows for conversation threads, links to articles, and a space for detailed analysis and argument.

- **Interaction and Engagement** : On X, interaction is more direct and political. Replies, RTs , and comments generate debate that is less common on other platforms. Additionally, X's algorithm favors content that generates discussion, which is vital for politics.

ANALYZING TRUMP'S VICTORY IN X: THE UNDISPUTED INFLUENCE OF THE PLATFORM ON POLITICS

Introduction

In this chapter, I seek to understand Donald Trump's victory in the context of X's influence, exploring how the platform can be a key determinant in modern elections. Trump and Kamala Harris's interaction on X during the US presidential election offers a revealing case study. My aim here is to demonstrate that X's influence cannot be separated from political outcomes and that the facts support this notion. I will analyse the engagement of both candidates to test this hypothesis, offering a lesson on how digital communication can be decisive in contemporary politics.

Analysis of Trump vs. Kamala in X

- **Trump vs. Kamala** : On the digital front, Trump had a resounding victory over Kamala Harris. His ability to engage was noticeably superior, suggesting his message resonated differently. Looking at the polls, it seemed like Kamala was close or even, but what was happening in X was a strong indication of the actual direction of support.

- **Understanding Current Politics** : The way people consume and understand politics has changed. Traditional polls do not capture this new landscape where the influence of social media is crucial. People can say one thing on the phone and think or act differently in the anonymity of social media.

- **Measuring Behavior** : As a political scientist, I understand that surveys must begin to consider these new digital variables. Political behavior is now more complex, and what happens on social media is an intimate and significant part of that behavior.

Trump and Kamala's X Data Analysis:

- **Trump:**

  o **Post 1 (November)** : 5K comments, 34K RTs , 152K likes, 11M views.

  o **Post 2 (November)** : 41K comments, 109K RTs , 689K likes, 63M views.

- **Kamala:**

  o **Post 1 (November 3)** : 15K comments, 25K RTs , 127K likes, 44M views.

  o **Post 2 (November)** : 4K comments, 8K RTs , 32K likes, 1M views.

Digital Impact Calculation:

To understand the impact of both candidates on X, I have applied the Total Value of Influence formula that values engagement over the number of followers:

Formula:

- Total Value = (Followers × 0.10) + (RTs × 0.40) + (Comments × 0.30) + (Likes × 0.10) + (Views × 0.10)

Donald Trump:

- **Followers** : 95.9 million (although we will not use this number directly for the calculation, it is important for context).

- **Post 1:**

  o Comments: 5,000 × 0.30 = 1,500

  o RTs : 34,000 × 0.40 = 13,600

  o Likes: 152,000 × 0.10 = 15,200

  o Views: 11,000,000 × 0.10 = 1,100,000

Total Value Post 1 : 1,500 + 13,600 + 15,200 + 1,100,000 = **1,130,300**

- **Post 2:**

  o Comments: 41,000 × 0.30 = 12,300

  o RTs : 109,000 × 0.40 = 43,600

  o Likes: 689,000 × 0.10 = 68,900

  o Views: 63,000,000 × 0.10 = 6,300,000

  Total Value Post 2 : 12,300 + 43,600 + 68,900 + 6,300,000 = **6,424,800**

  Trump's Posts Average:

- (1,130,300 + 6,424,800) / 2 = **3,777,550**

  Kamala Harris:

- **Followers : Not provided, but we will use the same** engagement approach .

- **Post 1:**

  o Comments: 15,000 × 0.30 = 4,500

  o RTs : 25,000 × 0.40 = 10,000

  o Likes: 127,000 × 0.10 = 12,700

  o Views: 44,000,000 × 0.10 = 4,400,000

  Total Value Post 1 : 4,500 + 10,000 + 12,700 + 4,400,000 = **4,427,200**

- **Post 2:**

  o Comments: 4,000 × 0.30 = 1,200

  o RTs : 8,000 × 0.40 = 3,200

- Likes: $32,000 \times 0.10 = 3,200$

- Views: $1,000,000 \times 0.10 = 100,000$

Total Value Post 2 : $1,200 + 3,200 + 3,200 + 100,000 =$ **107,600**

Harris Posts Average:

- $(4,427,200 + 107,600) / 2 =$ **2,267,400**

Comparative and Conclusions:

When comparing the values, it is evident that Trump significantly outperformed Harris in terms of engagement on X. This numerical analysis reflects:

1. **Direct and Amplified Communication** : Trump used X to communicate directly with his base, generating engagement that far exceeded his opponent. This level of interaction translates into direct political influence over voters.

2. **Speed and Reach** : Trump's ability to rapidly spread his messages, with posts generating millions of views, demonstrates how X enables immediate and massive reach, affecting political perception and support.

3. **Relevance of Engagement** : The high rate of RTs and comments for Trump shows that his content was not only being viewed but also inciting action – sharing and discussion – which is crucial for moving votes and opinions.

4. **Impact on the Election Outcome** : Trump's digital dominance on X was a harbinger of his victory at the polls, indicating that traditional measures of voting intention could be outdated if they do not consider the flow of information and opinion on platforms like X.

For these reasons, I am convinced that X exerts a remarkable influence on contemporary politics, redefining how candidates communicate, how voters form their opinions, and ultimately how elections are decided.

Engagement Rate

X's influence on modern politics is undeniable, and in this chapter, I break down how this platform has redefined political communication through the metric of engagement . Using engagement data from Donald Trump and Kamala Harris during the US presidential election, we can better understand how X impacts the political landscape.

Engagement Rate Calculation :

To calculate the Engagement Rate (ER), we use the following formula:

- ER = (Total Interactions / Number of Followers) × 100

Donald Trump:

- **Followers** : 95.9 million

- **Post 1:**

  o Total Interactions: Comments (5,000) + RTs (34,000) + Likes (152,000) = 191,000

  o ER = (191,000 / 95,900,000) × 100 ≈ **0.20%**

- **Post 2:**

  o Total Interactions: Comments (41,000) + RTs (109,000) + Likes (689,000) = 839,000

  o ER = (839,000 / 95,900,000) × 100 ≈ **0.88%**

Engagement Rate :

- (0.20% + 0.88%) / 2 = **0.54%**

Kamala Harris:

- **Followers** : Not provided, but we'll assume a ballpark number for the calculation. We'll use 10 million as a conservative estimate to illustrate the engagement rate , as exact followers can vary but the number is necessary for the formula.

- **Post 1:**

  - Total Interactions: Comments (15,000) + RTs (25,000) + Likes (127,000) = 167,000

  - ER = (167,000 / 10,000,000) × 100 = **1.67%**

- **Post 2:**

  - Total Interactions: Comments (4,000) + RTs (8,000) + Likes (32,000) = 44,000

  - ER = (44,000 / 10,000,000) × 100 = **0.44%**

Harris Engagement Rate Average :

- (1.67% + 0.44%) / 2 = **1.055%**

Comparative and Conclusions

- **Relative Engagement** : Even though Trump has a significantly larger number of followers, his engagement rate is lower compared to Harris. This suggests that for each follower, Harris generates more interaction, although Trump achieves higher absolute engagement due to the larger follower base.

- **Political Influence** : Harris' high engagement rate could indicate a message that resonates more with her audience, although in absolute terms, Trump generates more overall engagement due to his base of followers.

- **Electoral Impact** : Trump's digital win could be attributed more to the number of total interactions than the engagement rate . This reflects how X can amplify a message to a mass audience, regardless of the engagement rate per follower.

- **Relevance of X** : This analysis shows how X is not only a means of communicating, but can be a predictor of political influence when viewed through the lens of engagement . Candidates who manage to mobilize their followers to actively interact with their content can influence public opinion and, potentially, election outcomes.

Engagement on X, therefore, offers valuable insight into political impact, showing that it matters not only how many people follow a candidate, but how and to what extent they interact with their messages .

Both calculations are important

The logic behind X's influence on politics lies in its ability to democratize, accelerate and amplify political communication. Let's break down this logic through concrete data on Donald Trump and Kamala Harris' engagement during the US presidential election.

Engagement Rate Calculation Logic :

- **Engagement Concept : The** engagement rate (ER) in X is crucial because it not only measures the number of interactions but how these interactions relate to the follower base. It is a metric that reflects the effectiveness of a political message in capturing and retaining attention.

- **Engagement Rate Formula** : ER = (Total Interactions / Number of Followers) × 100. This formula allows us to compare the intensity of engagement across different accounts, regardless of their size.

Donald Trump:

- **Follower Base** : With 95.9 million followers, Trump has a massive audience to engage with.

- **Interactions vs. Followers** : Although Trump generates a high number of interactions, his engagement rate is relatively low due

77

to his large follower base. This indicates a wide reach but a lower proportional engagement per follower.

- o **Post 1** : ER $\approx 0.20\%$

- o **Post 2** : ER $\approx 0.88\%$

- o **Average** : 0.54%

Kamala Harris:

- **Follower Base** : We assume a follower base of 10 million for illustrative purposes, although the actual number may vary.

- **Interactions vs. Followers : Harris shows a higher** engagement rate , suggesting that although her audience is smaller, it is more active or that her content generates more interaction per follower.

- o **Post 1** : ER = 1.67%

- o **Post 2** : ER = 0.44%

- o **Average** : 1.055%

Logic of Political Impact:

- **Message Amplification** : Trump, with his huge audience, can achieve massive impact in absolute terms, even with a relatively low engagement rate . His success on X shows how a broad base can translate into greater visibility and, potentially, political influence.

- **Engagement Quality** : Harris, with a higher engagement rate , may be connecting more deeply with a smaller audience, indicating that message quality and audience relevance may be more important than audience size suggests.

- **Influence on the Elections** : Trump's victory in the digital arena was not necessarily based on the engagement rate but on the ability to generate a high number of total interactions, which translates into greater reach and, therefore, greater influence on public discourse and voter mobilization.

- **Transformation of Political Communication** : X has changed the logic of political communication by allowing direct and constant interaction between candidates and voters, overcoming the limitations of time and space that traditional media had.

- **Measuring Influence :** Engagement rates give us a measure of how politicians are resonating with their audiences, providing a more nuanced perspective on influence that can't be captured with traditional surveys.

In conclusion, the logic of X's influence on politics is based on the platform's ability to transform the reach, speed and intensity of the political message, making this social network an indispensable tool for understanding and directing public opinion in the 21st century.

Chapter: Resolving the Discrepancy between Engagement Rate and Absolute Engagement

In my analysis of influence on X, I have observed a significant discrepancy between two key metrics: engagement rate and absolute engagement . Here I explain how I have addressed this dilemma in my studies.

The Weighted Average:

To balance this discrepancy, I have chosen to use a weighted average. I have assigned weights based on the relevance of each metric for the analysis of political influence:

Engagement (60%): This weighting reflects the importance of mass reach and the ability of a message to be amplified at a macro level.

Engagement Rate (40%): Here, the weight recognizes the intensity of the connection with the audience, indicating how each follower interacts with the content.

To calculate this weighted average, I have used concrete examples:

If my absolute engagement is 1,000,000 interactions and my engagement rate is 2%, the weighted score would be:

$(1,000,000 * 0.60) + (2 * 0.40) = 600,000 + 0.8 = 600,008$

Combined Influence Index:

I have normalized this data to make it comparable:

Engagement : If the maximum possible absolute engagement is 10 million interactions, then 1,000,000 is 10%.

Engagement Rate : If the maximum for the rate is 10%, then 2% is 20%.

Sum of normalized indices:

10% (Absolute Engagement) + 20% (Engagement Rate) = 30% combined influence.

Context Analysis:

I have learned that context is crucial:

In campaigns that seek to mobilize large voter bases, absolute engagement is my main focus.

Where I'm looking for a deeper connection with a specific audience, engagement rate is my guide.

Segmentation and Comparison:

My methodology includes:

Segment by Content Type: I look at how different types of posts affect both metrics, providing a more detailed view of my influence.

Temporal or Campaign Comparison: I evaluate how these metrics fluctuate over time or between campaigns, identifying patterns and trends.

Hybrid Metrics:

I have created a hybrid metric for my analysis:

Engagement Index : This metric is calculated as the product of absolute engagement by the engagement rate , offering a combined view of reach and depth of interaction.

Final Considerations:

Alignment with Objective: My choice of method is always based on the objectives of my analysis. If I am looking to understand the loyalty of my audience, the engagement rate is my North Star. If my goal is to measure the impact on public opinion, absolute engagement is my North Star.

Iteration and Adjustment: My approach is not static. I adjust weights and methods as I obtain more data and refine my objectives.

Using this methodology, I have gained a more holistic understanding of my influence on X, mitigating the limitations of relying solely on one metric and thus offering a more nuanced view of my digital impact.

Application of the Methodology to Balance the Discrepancy between Engagement Rate and Absolute Engagement

I applied a weighting methodology to address the discrepancy between engagement rate and absolute engagement , using Donald Trump and Kamala Harris data in X. Here are the details of this analysis:

Initial Data:

- **Donald Trump** :
  - Engagement Rate : 0.54%
  - Engagement Average: 3,777,550
- **Kamala Harris** :
  - Engagement Rate : 1.055%
  - Engagement Average: 2,267,400

Engagement Weighting :

I have decided to weight these metrics as follows:
- **Absolute Engagement** : 60%
- **Engagement Rate** : 40%

Calculation for Trump:

- **Weighted Absolute Engagement** : 3,777,550 * 0.60 = 2,266,530
- **Weighted Engagement Rate** : 0.54 * 0.40 = 0.216

Trump Weighted Average:

- **Normalized Influence Value (NIV)** : (2,266,530 / 3,777,550) * 0.60 + (0.54 / 1.055) * 0.40 ≈ 0.6 + 0.2044 = **0.8044**

Calculation for Harris:

- **Weighted Absolute Engagement** : 2,267,400 * 0.60 = 1,360,440
- **Weighted Engagement Rate** : 1.055 * 0.40 = 0.422

Harris Weighted Mean:

- Harris **VIN : (2,267,400 / 3,777,550) * 0.60 + (1.055 / 1.055) * 0.40 ≈ 0.36 + 0.4 = 0.76**

Combined Influence Index:

To normalize and combine this data, I used Trump's values as a reference for normalization:

- **Trump** :
    - Engagement : 3,777,550 / 3,777,550 = 1
    - Engagement Rate : 0.54 / 1.055 = 0.511
    - **VIN** : 1 * 0.60 + 0.511 * 0.40 = **0.8044**
- **Harris** :
    - Engagement : 2,267,400 / 3,777,550 ≈ 0.6
    - Engagement Rate : 1.055 / 1.055 = 1
    - **VIN** : 0.6 * 0.60 + 1 * 0.40 = **0.76**

Hybrid Metrics:

- **Engagement Index for Trump** :
    - 3,777,550 * 0.54 = **2,039,857**
- **Engagement Index for Harris** :
    - 2,267,400 * 1.055 = **2,392,007**

Interpretation of Results:

- **Weighted Average** : Trump scores higher due to his significant ability to generate absolute engagement , which is vital in campaigns seeking mass reach. However, the weighting also recognizes the importance of engagement rate .
- **Combined Influence Index** : Trump leads in this index due to his high reach, although Harris has a higher engagement rate per follower. This shows how the weighting balances between reach and resonance.
- **Effective Engagement Index** : Harris outperforms Trump on this index, indicating that although her absolute reach was smaller, her message generated more intense engagement with her audience.

Engagement Data :

To ensure transparency in my analysis:

- **Data Collection** : I selected the two posts from each candidate published on November 3, choosing those with the highest interactions to reflect the maximum impact of their communication that day.
- **Additional Observations** : Trump's consistency in generating high engagement , with views always above a million, contrasts with the variability of Harris, whose engagement fluctuates more.
- **Transparency and Objectivity** : I have avoided bias, focusing on metrics that reflect the maximum impact of each candidate on X.
- **Verification** : Data is available on the X feed for anyone to review, ensuring the accuracy and transparency of my analysis.

Conclusion on the Methodology:

This methodology allows us to see both the potential for influence of each candidate and the variability in their engagement . By weighting absolute engagement and engagement rate , we get a more balanced view of how both aspects contribute to political influence in X, recognizing both the capacity for mass mobilization and the depth of the connection with the audience.

APPLICATION OF THE METHODOLOGY TO BALANCE THE DISCREPANCY BETWEEN ENGAGEMENT RATE AND ABSOLUTE ENGAGEMENT FOR MARÍA CORINA MACHADO AND NICOLÁS MADURO

Note on Data Used:

For this analysis, I have taken as a sample 2 posts published by each of the candidates on the date of July 30, 2024.

Initial Data:

Nicolas Maduro:
- **Followers** : 4.8 million
- **Post 1 (July 30, 2024)** :
  - o Comments: 4
  - o RTs : 3,000
  - o Likes: 5,000
  - o Views: 1,000,000
- **Post 2 (July 30, 2024)** :
  - o Comments: 5,000
  - o RTs : 3,000
  - o Likes: 6,000
  - o Views: 1,000,000

Maria Corina Machado:
- **Followers** : 6 million
- **Post 1 (July 30, 2024)** :
  - o Comments: 5,000
  - o RTs : 76,000
  - o Likes: 300,000
  - o Views: 12,000,000
- **Post 2 (July 30, 2024)** :
  - o Comments: 9,000

- o RTs : 61,000
- o Likes: 291,000
- o Views: 9,000,000

Methodology:

1. **Metric Normalization:**

   - o **Maximum Absolute Engagement Observed** : 12,000,000 (Views of Machado Post 1).
   - o **Maximum Observed Engagement Rate** : 6.25% (Machado Post 1).

For Maduro:
   - o **Engagement (EAN) Post 1** : (1,000,000 / 12,000,000) = 0.0833
   - o **Engagement Rate (TEN) Post 1** : (0.17% / 6.25%) = 0.0272
   - o **EAN Post 2** : (1,000,000 / 12,000,000) = 0.0833
   - o **TEN Post 2** : (0.29% / 6.25%) = 0.0464

For Machado:
   - o **EAN Post 1** : (12,000,000 / 12,000,000) = 1
   - o **TEN Post 1** : (6.25% / 6.25%) = 1
   - o **EAN Post 2** : (9,000,000 / 12,000,000) = 0.75
   - o **TEN Post 2** : (5.91% / 6.25%) = 0.9456

2. **Weighing:**

We use a weighting of 60% for Absolute Engagement and 40% for Engagement Rate :

   - o **Formula for Normalized Influence Value (VIN)** :
     - ■ VIN = (EAN × 0.60) + (TEN × 0.40)

Calculation for Maduro:

- **VIN Post 1** : $(0.0833 * 0.60) + (0.0272 * 0.40) = 0.05 + 0.0109 = \mathbf{0.0609}$
- **VIN Post 2** : $(0.0833 * 0.60) + (0.0464 * 0.40) = 0.05 + 0.0186 = \mathbf{0.0686}$

Calculation for Machado:

- **VIN Post 1** : $(1 * 0.60) + (1 * 0.40) = 0.6 + 0.4 = \mathbf{1}$
- **VIN Post 2** : $(0.75 * 0.60) + (0.9456 * 0.40) = 0.45 + 0.3782 = \mathbf{0.8282}$

Interpretation of Results:

- **Mature** : With very low VINs , it reflects that, although it has a significant reach due to its follower base, its ability to generate active engagement is limited. This could indicate a less engaged audience or a communication strategy that fails to resonate or motivate. into action.
- **Machado** : Their VINs are much higher, showing significant influence on both metrics. The high engagement rate suggests that their content connects strongly with their audience, mobilizing participation and discussion.

Conclusions:

This methodology allows to balance the discrepancy between absolute engagement and engagement rate , offering a more holistic view of influence on X. While Maduro has a considerable presence in terms of followers and views, Machado excels in the ability to generate significant interaction, which is vital for political influence. This analysis highlights how, in modern politics, the effectiveness of a message is not only measured by its reach but also by how that message is received and responded to by the audience.

POLITICS IN THE DIGITAL AGE - RISKS AND POSSIBILITIES

The political fate of those who fail to get off to a good start on X is a constant subject of intrigue. In a world where direct communication and engagement are the currency of exchange, relevance on this platform can be a decisive factor in anyone's political career. But can we trust that X influencers have the ability to transcend the digital world into electoral success? The example of Donald Trump is exceptional, but it is worth remembering that he was already a celebrity before his presidency, which gave him an inherent advantage.

When I evaluate those numbers going up and down, depending on the moment, the behavior of the subject and how it is perceived, it becomes clear that the values in X are volatile. If the values change, if the public feels that it no longer represents them, this is reflected harshly in the network, showing an unprecedented dynamic. There are no longer filters of traditional media; X's new algorithm has removed that filter, and as Elon Musk says, "the news is you," and you can be the star if you want to be.

This new reality is so new that it hasn't fully sunk in yet, and we'll no doubt see surprises. Can we be stars both on X and in real life? Trump is, others are, but doing so takes significant effort.

X and the Relevance of CCOs:

Elon Musk and X have given unprecedented importance to Original Content Creators (OCCs), especially when it comes to videos. Here lies a fundamental truth: political influence on X depends largely on how well a content creator knows how to use the tools available. You can just write and give your opinion on the news, which is a first step on the ladder of connecting with people, but this is not enough.

Going from being a simple user to reaching a higher level, as is the case with video, is where the real challenge lies, but also the path to

89

something more tangible and to politics. Recording and presenting your side of the story shows that you are a real human being, speaking and expressing your opinion in front of others. Doing this with quality means that X's algorithm understands it and rewards you by giving you a recommendation space, reaching tens, hundreds of thousands, and even millions of people. This is the core of X's algorithm, and video is the apex.

Combining a well-written post that is read while the viewer watches the video is the magic that takes you to the top as a CCO. That is where you need to be, with all that digital industry at your disposal, with applications that understand that you are a winner and will take you to the Olympus of influencers , where you will reign. Of course, this requires being bold; saying and being relevant in X requires courage, honesty and will, because political issues can be strong and facing them, as has been the case when confronting Maduro, requires brave people.

My Personal Experience:

Personally, I have needed a psychological change that has led me to understand my commitment to the people, to those who suffer, to the people who believe in me and want me to transmit the truth, the message of hope, the solution, and for all of this to become a digital embrace of strength. X understands this, and that is why this network is the depth of politics, and politics is a fundamental part of our lives. That is where success lies: whoever wins in X, wins on the physical plane of politics.

Conclusion:

Believe in what you do, do your best, and you will overcome the barrier to become one of those who walk in X with the force of influence. Politics in the digital age is not just about having followers; it is about how you connect with them, how you speak to them, and how you use the tools at your disposal to transform that digital connection into real impact. The pinnacle of being a CCO in X, with video as the main tool, is the path to tangible influence and victory in politics.

RESISTANCE IN IMAGES: THE POWER OF AI IN POLITICAL COMMUNICATION

Today, seeing the AI-generated image of X that captures the essence of Venezuela's struggle against oppression, I can't help but feel deeply moved. This image, which shows a child, a symbol of our country's hope and future, bravely facing the figure of Maduro, bound by chains but still resilient, is a powerful reminder of our reality and our unbreakable spirit.

AI has not only captured the confrontation, but it has also captured the clamor of the Venezuelan people through the raised hands in the background, a collective cry for freedom and justice. This act of image generation is not just a technological achievement; it is a demonstration of AI's potential to amplify and visualize the political and social narratives that define our struggle.

The political adaptation of communication is crucial, especially in times where information is power. Social media, and X in particular, have become the arena where the battle for truth and public perception is fought. AI, with its ability to interpret and represent collective sentiment, becomes a tool vital for social and political movements. It allows us not only to communicate, but also to connect, mobilize and educate on an unprecedented scale. However, this image speaks to us of something deeper. It tells us that the problem we face with Maduro is not something we are going to leave for future generations, but is a crisis that demands immediate action.

This image symbolizes the transition from the old to the new, from oppression to liberation. AI is telling us that what is coming for Venezuela is not the continuation of the last 25 years under Chavismo, but a change driven by the consciousness of the people. This child in the image represents Venezuela in its state of childhood, awakening. He is a brave child who does not bow down to Maduro, who does not fear Maduro because he wants to be free. Here, the child is resistance itself, symbolizing those new actors of change who are not afraid to confront the tyrant on his own ground.

This representation reminds us that the fight for freedom and justice in Venezuela is not just a question of politics, but of humanity, of not allowing oppression to become normalized. AI, in its capacity to generate and process information, becomes an ally in this fight, helping us visualize and communicate the resistance, hope, and future that we all want for Venezuela.

It is imperative that we use these tools not only to document our history, but also to forge our future, one where freedom of expression and respect for human rights are the norm, not the exception. This image, then, is more than art; it is a declaration of intent, a digital battle cry that reminds us that the fight continues, and that, in every brave child, in every raised hand, there is a Venezuela that aspires to be free.

Esteban Oria, December 2024

EPILOGUE

In this book, we have navigated the complex ecosystem of digital influence, looking at how social network X has redefined politics and leadership. From Donald Trump's high-profile victory in the US presidential election to the intricate political landscape of Venezuela, we have analyzed how figures such as Trump, María Corina Machado, and Nicolás Maduro have exploited the capabilities of X to shape public perception and political narrative.

We have developed a **comprehensive formula to calculate Total Influence Value** in X, which not only considers the follower base but also the depth of interaction with the shared content:

- **Total Influence Value** = (Followers × 0.10) + (RTs × 0.40) + (Comments × 0.30) + (Likes × 0.10) + (Views × 0.10).

This approach underlines that at X, true influence is measured by how engagement is generated , not merely by audience size. We have adjusted this formula to recognise the additional value of **Original Content Creators (OCCs)** and introduced **Engagement Rate (ER)** to assess how content resonates with audiences:

- **Engagement Rate** = (Total Interactions / Number of Followers) × 100.

The analysis has revealed that politics is now forged not just in rallies and headlines, but in every retweet , comment and like, proving that traditional polling must be adapted to capture the impact of social media on public opinion. Trump used X for direct communication and mass reach, showing that in the digital age, these strategies are as crucial as traditional campaigns.

However, we have also explored the **formulas and rates of deception** , highlighting how reach can be manipulated through bots or false information, particularly in the Venezuelan context. The deception rate measures genuine versus manipulated content, revealing how engagement on X can be artificially inflated, affecting political perception and reality.

We have classified the influence into categories from " Emerging Voices " to " Iconic Influencers ," based on the range of RTs per post, to understand how engagement reflects the potential for impact and change at different scales.

This book has not only been an analysis of data, but a reflection on the evolution of politics in the technological context. We have seen that influence on X is a complex interaction between followers and engagement , where leaders who understand these dynamics can powerfully influence public opinion. However, we have also warned about the need to be critical of manipulation tactics that can distort the digital truth.

In conclusion, X does not just reflect politics; it shapes it, offering both opportunities and challenges for more direct, democratic and effective communication, while reminding us of the need to discern between authentic influence and digital deception in our age.

Follow me on my X account **@estebanoria**

www.ingramcontent.com/pod-product-compliance
Lightning Source LLC
LaVergne TN
LVHW051716050326
832903LV00032B/4239